FIRST EDITION

SCHOENHUT DOLLS & TOYS

A Loving Legacy

by

SUSAN MANOS

D1519600

COLLECTOR BOOKS

A Division of Schroeder Publishing Co., Inc.

P.O. BOX 3009 • PADUCAH, KENTUCKY 42001

Additional copies of this book may be ordered
@$8.95 postpaid from
COLLECTOR BOOKS
P.O. Box 3009
Paducah, Kentucky   42001

Printed by Taylor Publishing Company, Dallas, Texas

SCHOENHUT DOLLS & TOYS

A Loving Legacy

Table of Contents

A LOVING LEGACY — SCHOENHUT DOLLS AND TOYS
Susan Manos

DEDICATED TO
MY DAUGHTER, CAROL,
AND TO THE YOUNG AT HEART

ACKNOWLEDGMENTS

Dolls are objects of love. Love is a feeling of affection, fondness and warm regard . . . This is what I feel toward all who have helped to make this book possible.

THANK YOU:
Margaret Haley, for your encouragement
Patricia Smith
Donna Stanley
Patricia Quinn, black and white photography
Churikian and Schlossberg, color photography
Dwight Smith, photography
Gladys Laurie
And all collectors and dealers throughout the U.S. for price guidance in all areas. Without you, this book would have remained a dream.

All items in this book are in the personal collection of Susan Manos.

COVER: Schoenhut Doll Crib and five different Schoenhut babies.
Humpty Dumpty Circus Clowns and Acrobat. Felix the Cat, Negro Rolly Dolly and Schoenhut Cat.

Introduction
by
GLADYS HILL HILLSDORF

A friend to all doll collectors.

Susan Manos is a tall, vibrant, handsome woman whose enthusiasm for research and love of dolls inspires all who come in contact with her.

Perhaps her love of dolls stems from the fact that she wanted children of her own so badly and had been denied that privilege for fourteen and one-half years. When her lovely Carol was born, her joy was beyond belief.

Susan operates a museum on the lower level of her home where all are welcome, especially children. Her dolls are dolls that have been played with and she has a well-rounded collection. Her little daughter shares her mother's love and Carol has her own little museum on the top floor. Carol is talented and at the age of seven years was modeling her own dolls, which were amazingly good. (Called the Carol Doll.)

Susan has spent money and long hours on the research of Schoenhuts and all of the information in this book is authentic.

Susan's husband, Paris, like all husbands of doll collectors, has been very patient.

Susan spends much of her time giving talks at museums, schools and fund-raising for Church groups. Her personality shines through the pages of this book and I know that you will enjoy it as much as I have.

Foreword

The name Schoenhut is a magic one. The *SCHOEN-HUT WORLD,* filled with dolls, toys, animals, musical instruments, blocks, doll houses, circus figures, games, etc., is synonymous with the words *HAPPI-NESS, JOY AND LOVE.* Albert Schoenhut created this *WORLD* with the child in mind. With his loving contribution, he sparked the creative imagination in many a child and was indeed a true artist. The Schoenhut Creations of yesterday are with us today, not only within our hearts but as much sought-after works of art. Albert Schoenhut has left us a *LOVING LEGACY.*

The *SCHOENHUT WORLD* began in the third quarter of the 19th Century with the creation of a toy piano. These beginnings were the foundation upon which Albert Schoenhut created even more toys and dolls that focused upon the psychological development of the child. Schoenhut means *CREATIVITY.* You will surely share my enthusiasm for the *SCHO-ENHUT WORLD* as you follow the history of the Family and view many of the original Schoenhut Dolls and Toys through the art of photography in *"THE SCHOENHUT DOLLS AND TOYS — A LOVING LEG-ACY."*

ALBERT SCHOENHUT, FOUNDER

Albert Schoenhut, son of Frederick and grandson of Anton, both toymakers from Wurtemburg, Germany, was born on February 5, 1849, in Goeppengein, Germany. At age 17, he arrived in the United States to settle in Philadelphia. It was 1866 and right after the close of the Civil War. Albert did not enter the United States as an immigrant, cold and bewildered, but came under the aegis of Mr. Dahl, the buyer for the large store of Wanamakers & Sons.

Albert's first job at Wanamakers was the repair of the glass sounding pieces in toy pianos. He saw that these glass sounding pieces were totally unsatisfactory and he invented the metal sounding bars.

It was during the year 1872 that Albert, now 23 years old, with wife Emilie and their eight children (six sons and two daughters), struck out on his own to invent his own toy piano. This perfected piano is described in another section of this book. The piano was an instant success. It reflected the ingenuity and designs of the inventor, and Albert began a thriving business for the Schoenhut Family.

Albert Schoenhut left a Germany that was feudal by demand and nature in its outlook and discipline. Because of his early training and background, he too demanded respect and no questions from his children. His organization was run as tightly as a smoothly operated military machine and each son entered the business at posts designated by their father. He was the patriarch, the ruler, the head of the family and business.

This feudalization was tempered by his great love of children. He had a knack of understanding their needs, particularly in the world of toys.

Some of the first toys made by Schoenhut were the two circus clowns, Humpty and Dumpty. This was a time of the big circuses such as Ringling and P. T. Barnum; it was the days of Buffalo Bill Cody and the Great Side Shows and Freaks. It was a time when the traveling circus sparked the imagination of all children.

Humpty and Dumpty was patented, along with the Humpty Dumpty Circus, in the U.S., Germany and Britain in 1903. As demand grew, so did the Schoenhut Circus. Figures were added — the Lady Acrobat, Lion Tamer, Ring Master, Gent Acrobat, Lady Circus Rider. Although these figures were identical, they came with different clothes. They also came with both bisque and wooden heads. To complete the circus, the figures of Negro Dude, Chinaman Acrobat and Hobo Clown were added.

1907 brought the introduction of two lovable characters, Max and Moritz, two German boys. They were followed by the Farmer and Milkmaid in the Farm Set and then Mary Had A Little

Lamb Set. The Rolly Dollys, patented in 1908, came in a great many designs. Although these were patented much earlier (1902), they reached success around 1908.

A 53 piece set named "Teddy's Adventures in Africa" was put on the market and included several new dolls. The finest of this set was a true portrait of Teddy Roosevelt. This was the first spring jointed doll made by Schoenhut. Many of the animals that went with the "Teddy" Set are thought to belong to the well-known Circus Set.

On July 3, 1909, Albert Schoenhut filed a patent application for a wooden doll. This patent was not granted until January 17, 1911. The patent covered a complicated mechanism consisting of steel spring hinges, heavy double spring tension and swivel connections. No rubber to loosen or break existed. These dolls could be placed in a natural position, a position which the human body could assume. They were made entirely of wood, painted with enamel oil colors and were very artistically proportioned. Two holes in the soles of the feet fitted on posts in a metal disc and helped them to stand firmly.

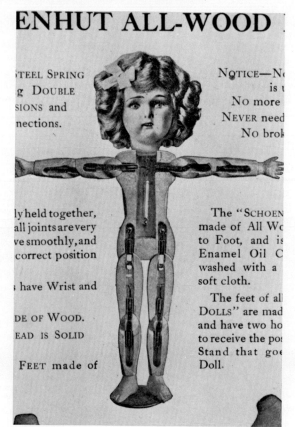

These dolls were boys, girls and babies. Some had wigs, some had carved and painted hair, some had ribbons and caps, others had set-in glass eyes, some intaglio or painted eyes. They came in four sizes: 14", 16", 19" and 21". The babies came in sizes of 9", 11", 14", 16", 19" and 21". They came in sixty different styles.

The clothing for these dolls was of the style of the period and could be considered a period costume doll. The dresses and underwear, done in the style of the time, were both elaborate and some were also made which were less expensive. They very accurately reflected the children's clothing of those days.

Prior to 1911, character dolls constructed entirely of wood were being imported to America. On May 1, 1911, Albert Schoenhut's sample dolls were ready for the toy trade. The "All Wood Perfection Art Dolls" were an instant success and orders came in, not only from American toy buyers but from Germany, France and Britain.

Of the first issue dolls, the two most popular were Tootsie Wootsie, a baby, and a toddler called Schnickel-Fritz, who had a smile that included two upper and two lower teeth.

In December this same year (1911), Albert Schoenhut advertised a doll based on the cartoons of Herbert Johnson, Mr. Common People, and by 1912, Carrie (Top Knot Lady), with molded ribbon heads and molded bonnets heads came on the market.

The production of dolls continued until 1926. After 1911, Schoenhut gave his dolls numbers rather than names although orders included code words. No. 106, a boy with molded cap, was coded as "Deadly." All these code names began with the letter "D."

Albert Schoenhut became a member of Toy Manufacturers' Association of U.S.A. and used a seal showing that his toys were made in the U.S. The seal, appearing in many magazine ads, was an Uncle Sam hat, with brim side up. Toys, boats, dolls, houses, etc., extended out the top of the hat. Over it was a ribbon streamer with "Toy Mfr's U.S.A." and across the lower part of the hat it stated "American Toys." (Refer to picture in "OTHER TOYS" Section.)

Between 1872 and 1912, toys seemed to grow out of the Schoenhut Factory. Not only circus toys, dolls and pianos but delightful toys that filled the hands, heads and hearts of the children of those days. Such items as games, guns, blocks and musical instruments were produced.

In 1912, Albert Schoenhut died at the age of 63 and, due to his guidance and training, his six sons (Harry E., Gustav A., Theodore C., Albert F., William G. and Otto F.) continued to operate the Schoenhut business. The company was headed by Albert F. Schoenhut who continued his father's policies as far as he was able to do so.

It was in 1913 that the first infant dolls, called "Nature" Dolls, were placed on the market. They had curved legs and arms. The dolls' heads were designed and copyrighted by Harry E. Schoenhut. Prior to this, some of the heads had been sculptured by Adolph Graziana, an Italian, and some by an artist who went by the name Mr. Leslie.

These Nature Dolls first appeared with molded hair, but within a few months they came out with a Dutch style bobbed wig. This bent limb baby came in 9" and 11" sitting and 14" and 17" standing. Both the arms and legs of the bent limbs were made with two pieces of wood fitted together.

These heads were placed on fully jointed toddler bodies and also came in two sizes for each body style.

In 1915, a series of older toys were manufactured by the Schoenhut factory. Usually these dolls were dressed as athletes such as football, baseball and basketball players. They were 19" tall with jointed wrists. When found undressed, they are often referred to as "mannequins."

In 1915, the Schoenhut factory increased in size and moved from 2445 to 2465 Sepviva Street in Philadelphia. In 1917, the Schoenhuts hired Mrs. Katherine A. Rauser to be Couturier of their dolls. 1919 was the year the walking dolls were introduced. They came in sizes 11", 14" and 17". These walking dolls did not have the holes in the soles and the shoes were made at a slight angle to help the doll walk. In 1920, William G. Schoenhut obtained a U.S. Patent for a decal film to be used in making doll eyes. In 1921, Harry E. Schoenhut obtained two U.S. Patents for movable eyes. From 1917 through 1934, doll houses and toy apartment houses were added to the line. 1923 brought forth the railroad station to be used with the wooden toy trains. Doll house furniture was added in 1928 and continued through 1934.

In 1924, Schoenhut brought out a "cheaper" line of dolls. These were called Bass-Wood Elastic Dolls which used rubber elastic instead of metal springs. This year also introduced cloth bodied dolls with a name, voice box, wooden head and hands. The heads were hollowed out to make them as light as possible. They came in sizes of 14" and 16". 1924 also saw the Maggie and Jiggs from the cartoon BRINGING UP FATHER. Although these wooden dolls were trademarked by George Borgfeldt, they were made by Schoenhut.

1925 was the year the Schoenhuts brought out their wooden infant head which closely resembled the Bye-Lo Baby.

Members of the Schoenhut Family are still in business and listed below are dates and addresses that reflect the growth and changes of this great German-American Family:

The A. Schoenhut Company
Philadelphia, Pennsylvania

1914   The A. Schoenhut Company
2445 Sepviva Street
Philadelphia, Pennsylvania

1915	The A. Schoenhut Company
	2465 Sepviva Street
	Philadelphia, Pennsylvania
1926	The A. Schoenhut Company
	2304 East Hagert Street
	Philadelphia, Pennsylvania
1935	O. Schoenhut, Inc.
to date	2406 E. Castor Avenue
	Philadelphia, Pennsylvania
	(Founded by Otto Schoenhut and his
	nephew George Schoenhut.)

The Schoenhut contribution to education is one that can be viewed with pride. This company pioneered many construction toys, model wood toys, blocks, etc.

It is an interesting fact that Patty Smith Hill, an instructor of kindergarten and pre-school teachers at Columbia University, invented and patented a large, heavy wooden building block. It was created to be used in pre-school and kindergarten classes to help the physical and mental development of the very young child. After looking for the right company, she considered the A. Schoenhut Company as the perfect manufacturer to produce her invention. Though this was not an extremely large selling item, hundreds of sets were made to supply the local schools. An interesting fact about Patty Smith Hill is that she was the one who wrote and patented the song "Happy Birthday to You."

The first Schoenhut Company ran until 1934. In 1935 came the founding of the O. Schoenhut Company. The founder was Otto Schoenhut and his nephew George Schoenhut.

The A. Schoenhut Company had gone into bankruptcy in 1934. The buildings were still unsold and Otto and George Schoenhut had access to office space. During this period Otto met Emily T. Myers, the designer of the Pinn Family Dolls, and her advisor, Olga Landquist. They had hoped to have A. Schoenhut Co. make the dolls but discovered to their dismay that A. Schoenhut Company was not longer viable. Otto talked them into letting him take on the dolls because he had no other employment at the time. This was in the summer of 1935 and it was at that time that George Schoenhut, grandson of Albert Schoenhut, joined Otto in the business with the investment of a little capital.

Otto and George Schoenhut received permission from the receivers of the A. Schoenhut Company to use one of the rooms in the old factory on East Hagert and Sepviva Streets in order to set up a manufacturing process to make the Pinn Family Dolls. They were able to operate there until cold weather set in; there was no heat in the building.

Meanwhile, Albert F. and his son, Fred C., and another man whose hobby was model railroads set up the Schoenhut Manufacturing Company to make toy pianos and model railroad equipment. The two Schoenhuts had achieved the rights to make pianos under the Schoenhut name. This permission was probably given to them by the creditors who owned everything at that time.

As cold weather approached, Otto became frantic for a place to operate. In an old carpet factory, also on Hagert Street and not more than three blocks from the original factory, he found a third floor loft which had been vacated by a fly-by-night candy factory. The former occupants had left the premises coated with marshmallow and chocolate which was infested with vermin. This was cleaned and Otto and George moved their operation there just before the other buildings were sold at auction. The original Schoenhut buildings were bought by the Philadelphia Wool Scouring Company and used as a warehouse. The copper dome and the flagpole with Santa Claus in a sled was removed by the new owners and presented to Otto. Otto later erected it on a later building. The Wool Scouring Company later sold the building to the city which tore down the entire structure and built a school.

O. Schoenhut, Inc. operated under a kind of partnership agreement which later became the corporation. Besides Otto and George, there were two others, Stockton Mortimer and Stanley Osborn, both Philco Mfg. Co. executives.

The manufacture of the Pinn Dolls was at best a home craft industry and they realized that other objects were needed for sale. The new items that were introduced ultimately included pass-time "Perf-O-Art," a game "Boddle Ball," a novelty wand for drum majorettes, "Dixie Doodle," and a game about the possible war (after the craze of Monopoly) called "Europe Marches." None of them were very successful.

Shortly thereafter, Eugene Levay came into the Schoenhut World. He had just returned from a European buying trip where he picked up a game that had become very popular in Hungary. There it had been known variously as "Marocco" and "Sirocco." Otto and George were unable to understand Eugene Levay's enthusiasm because to them it seemed as nothing more than old-fashioned "Jack Straws." He insisted it would be good. With the help of two artist friends, Frances M. Lichten, author of "Decorative Arts of Victoria's Era" and "Folk Art of Rural Pennsylvania," and Katherine Milhouse, author and illustrator of many children's books such as SNOW OVER BETHLEHEM, LOVINO, THE EGG TREE, etc., they developed a package and some directions for playing as well as advertising material. It moved slowly at first but caught on and they were unable to fill orders. Managers of chain stores even drove to the third floor ex-candy factory and demanded merchandise to take with them.

It should be evident by now that the game was one which swept the whole country — the game of "Four, Five, Six — Pick up Sticks." It swept all of the other items out of their small factory, including the Pinn Dolls.

It became impossible to handle anything but the Sticks. With the manufacture of the Pick Up Sticks it was "success gone wild."

Just before 1941, the Schoenhut Manufacturing Company filed for bankruptcy. They moved out and O. Schoenhut, Inc., became the occupants of 2046 East Castor Avenue where they continued to make the Sticks and Pianos.

I have been very fortunate in being able to obtain a few toys which were made by the O. Schoenhut firm and I think they retain the quality and interest of the earlier toys.

As you view the photography, you will see some of the interesting toys that have been produced and, of course, the Schoenhut piano which is still in production.

George Schoenhut left the O. Schoenhut, Inc., firm in 1947. The manager is now Mr. Robert Zimmer, son-in-law of Otto Schoenhut.

Albert Schoenhut and young
grandson George Schoenhut.

TOY PIANOS

The toy piano with metal sounding bars was the first of its kind and marked the beginning of the Albert Schoenhut business. Although it was a toy, it had all the qualities of a full-sized piano. It was constructed in a fashion with keys the same size as a full-sized piano. This helped the child learn fingering techniques properly.

These pianos were sold in toy shops and music stores. Forty-two different sizes and styles were produced. They ranged in price from fifty cents to twenty-five dollars. The larger pianos had adjustable or straight piano stools which were priced separately.

The pianos pictured in this book are just a few of the different kinds and sizes made at that time.

A Schoenhut piano can still be purchased in toy stores and they are still being sold in the United States by:

O. Schoenhut, Inc.
2046 E. Castor Avenue
Philadelphia, Penna.   19134

PRICING INFORMATION

The prices in this book are current ones and it must be remembered: THESE PRICES ARE FOR PERFECT, MINT, ORIGINAL SCHOENHUT ITEMS.

A re-painted, scuffed, broken or damaged item is REDUCED in price, according to the extent of the damage.

Wild animal cage. Carved hair boy and circus people.

Character faced girl shown with Mary and her Little Lamb.

All original boy shown with farm set.

Toddler boy shown with 3 Rolly Dolly toys and animals.

Baby Grand Piano, Miss Dolly Schoenhut and carved hair boy and girl.

Delvan Humpty Dumpty circus of 1952.

Early small sized Humpty Dumpty Circus figures and animal.

Reduced size of the Humpty Dumpty Circus.

The Schoenhut Golfer $275.00.
Made by The A. Schoenhut Co.

Railroad Station with Hobo clown.

Bisque head circus people and animals.

NEGRO Schoenhut man.
All original.

DOLL HOUSE FURNITURE:
Bathroom $35.00, Kitchen $35.00
and Livingroom $25.00.

ROLLER CHIMES PUSH TOY. $200.00.

Carrie as a child and doll look-a-like. Carved hair boy.

Spirit of Hollywood camera, with dolls and piano.

16″ Carved hair girl.
All original.

16″ Carved hair girl.
All original.

Part of the DELVAN Humpty Dumpty circus. 1952.

Original Circus set in original box.

Shows the original Humpty Dumpty donkey and the DELVAN donkey (right).

Shows an original Schoenhut clown and chair and the re-introduced DELVA clown and chair (left).

Shows the DELVAN (1952) elephant with an original Humpty Dumpty one.

Original Humpty Dumpty Circus sign. $75.00.

Rolly Dolly Toys.

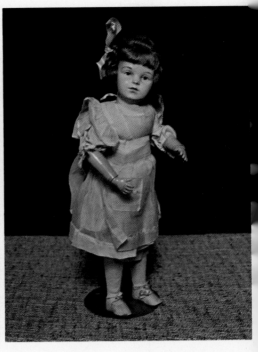

22″ all original somber faced girl.

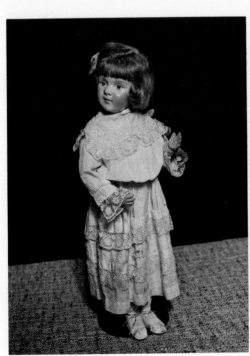

22″ Half smiling girl with a dimple in her chin, intaglio eyes and carved teeth. All original.

16″ Bonnet hatted girl.

Earlier Negro Dude in black. Later Negro Dude in natty colors.

Boy with smiling mouth and dimples. Has "squinty" eyes. Full mouth of carved teeth.

Carved hair boy in original baseball suit.

16" Walking Schoenhut.
All original.

16" Carved hair boy.

Man used in Stetson Hat ads.
22" and in his original underwear.

The A. Schoenhut Co. Trademark found on pianos and other musical instruments.

Large Baby Grand Piano $100.00. Single stool $75.00.

Double piano stool $100.00. Single piano stool $75.00.

Upright pianos. Large $85.00, Medium $65.00 and Small $55.00.

Large Upright Piano $100.00. Single stool $75.00.

HUMPTY DUMPTY-CIRCUS TOYS

Display Advertising Read:	**U.S. Patent**
Humpty Dumpty-Circus,	Dec. 2, 1902
Greatest Show on Earth,	Apr. 14, 1903
10,001 Different Tricks	May 17, 1904
	June 28, 1904
	Nov. 28, 1905
	Aug. 21, 1906
	Jan. 29, 1903
British Patent:	Jan. 12, 1903
Germany:	Apr. 21, 1903

This was the second group of toys introduced in 1902 to the market by A. Schoenhut Company.

Animals, circus personnel, tents, wagons, cages and miscellaneous items made up the Circus. These figures were made of solid wood and were unbreakable. They were jointed with heavy rubber cord and colored with enamel paint. Something interesting has been disclosed about the rubber cord used in the stringing: Apparently, the producer of the elastic used a different colored thread wrapping every year. The colors indicated the year of manufacture as a safeguard against unscrupulous claims for inferior merchandise. These colored elastic cords were used to determine the age of the figure if it were sent back for repairs.

Sets sold from seventy-five cents to twenty-five dollars according to the number of pieces in the set. Individual pieces sold from one cent for a balancing rod, to ninety cents for a lion, tiger, giraffe or buffalo.

Humpty Dumpty-Circus items were known to be made as late as 1926.

If items were not available at a dealer, they could be ordered by mail through free illustrated catalogs.

CATALOG REPRINT

Original HUMPTY DUMPTY CIRCUS. SMALL SET. Tent and 22 pieces: $1,500.00.

Early Humpty Dumpty Circus with glass eyed animals. Original box and poster. 22 piece set.
$2,000.00.

**BISQUE HEADS: LION TRAINER: $250.00. BARE BACK RIDER: $250.00. RING MASTER: $250.00.
STRONG MAN: $250.00.**

Lion Trainer (Wood Heads): $150.00. Ring Master: $175.00. Small Lion: $125.00.

Large early Negro DUDE in black coat and hat: $200.00.
Shorter panted one is later: $175.00.

Large Oriental ACROBAT: $175.00.

Large clown, silk suit: $85.00. Gray glass eyes Sea Lion: $200.00.
Brown, painted eyed Sea Lion: $175.00.

Large Clown, cotton suit: $75.00.

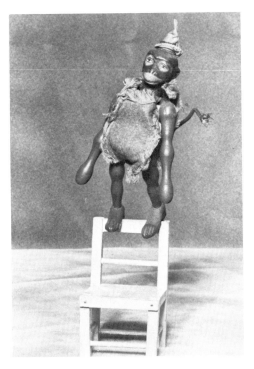

Yellow faced, smiling MONKEY: $225.00.　　　　Brown CHIMP type: $225.00.

Single hump CAMEL: GLASS EYES: $225.00. DECAL EYES: $200.00.

HIPPO with painted eyes: $200.00.

Glass eyed RHINO: $225.00.

Large Elephant with blanket and glass eyes: $200.00.

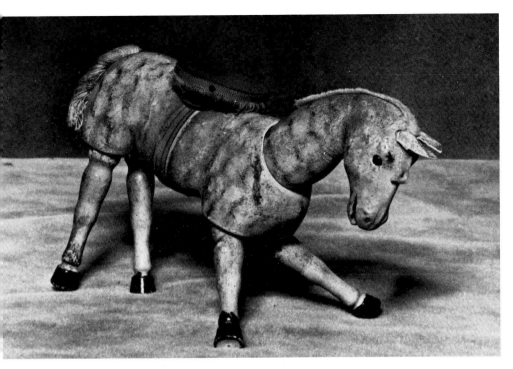

Large Platform Horse. Early glass eyed type: $200.00.

Large Donkey with blanket and glass eyes: $200.00.

Large Giraffe with painted eyes. $200.00.
Slightly smaller one with painted eyes.
$200.00.

Large Poodle with carved ruff. $175.00.
Reduced size Poodle with carved ruff, used
in smaller circus. $175.00.

Early type glass eyed poodle with a cloth ruff. $200.00.

Large Zebra with painted eyes. $200.00.

A rarer Burro with glass eyes. $225.00.

Polar Bear with glass eyes. $200.00.

Alligator with glass eyes. $225.00.

Leopard with glass eyes, open mouth with painted teeth. $225.00.

Cat with painted eyes. $200.00.

Buffalo with carved ruff. $250.00.

Earlier type Buffalo with glass eyes and cloth ruff. $200.00.

Smaller size brown bear. $125.00.

Elk with glass eyes. $200.00.
The deer has painted eyes and was a later addition to the set. $200.00.

Double hump CAMEL: LARGE: $200.00. SMALL: $150.00.

Large painted eyed Elephant: $150.00.

Brown Bear with glass eyes: $200.00.

Large Lion with carved mane: $200.00.

Circus props: $35.00 per set.

Wild Animal Circus Wagon Cage: $150.00. Small Lion: $125.00 and Large Tiger: $150.00.

Goat with glass eyes. $200.00.

Small carved mane horse with painted eyes. $150.00.

Large Riding Horse with glass eyes. Early type. $200.00.

Ostrich with glass eyes. $225.00.

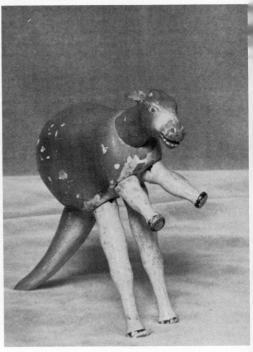

Kangaroo with glass eyes. $225.00.

OTHER TOYS
Produced from 1911 to 1934

Hundreds of other toys were manufactured by the company. Among the few are Modlwood Toys and all wood construction toys. They were made of unpainted wood and could be constructed and taken apart as well. The most popular were the Touring Car, Racing Car, Locomotive and Automobile, Schoenhut Toy guns for harmless target practice, military drilling, shooting sticks and rubber balls or paper caps. The guns were made of wooden barrels which made them free from danger. Shooting Gallery guns and target sets were popular toys for boys. Toy forts and cannons that could shoot rubber balls and corks, military equipment such as swords, helmets and knapsacks (in over twenty different U.S. styles) stimulated the minds of young boys.

There were still more: wooden sail boats, ukulele banjos, merry-go-round toys, roller chimes, walking wallapus, big game hunter, building blocks, metalophones, Naval war games, musical instruments and much more were produced by A. Schoenhut Company from 1911 to 1934.

Very few of these toys bore Schoenhut labels. Because of this it is difficult to identify them. Those that had the labels could be identified by the Schoenhut Trade Mark which was a large letter S in a circle with Glockenspiel or Metalophone and an elf tooting a horn in the center of the large letter.

These toys could be purchased from toy shops, department stores or ordered directly from the factory.

So much more could be written about the thousands of different toys produced by the A. Schoenhut Company, Schoenhut Manufacturing Company and O. Schoenhut, Inc., but pictures speak louder than words. You will view many of these later in the book.

Seal used by the A. Schoenhut Co. to help the sale of toys made in the U.S.A., after World War 1.

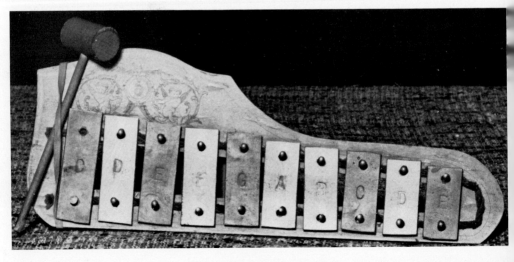

Earlier Metalophone $75.00.

Elfy Blocks, part of original set. 9 pieces: $65.00.

Naval War Toy game. Small ship shoots wooden pellets at target of Battleship and when hit, all parts fly in the air. Original box: $100.00.

Little Tots Building Blocks. Original box. $85.00.

ARCO TOP made by the O. Schoenhut Inc. $10.00.

"OLE" MILLION FACE game with over 1001 different changeable faces. $100.00.

Albert Schoenhut Co. "Spirit Of Hollywood" camera. Original box. $60.00.

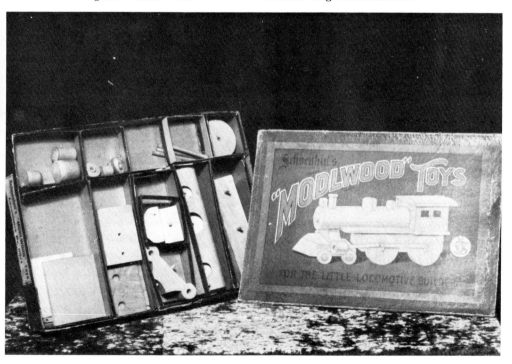

Early "Modlwood" toy locomotive. Original box. $100.00.

Trinity Chimes. $100.00.

FARM SET: FARMER: $175.00. MILK MAID: $175.00. COW (glass eyes): $200.00. DONKEY (glass eyes): $100.00. PIG (painted eyes): $85.00. GOOSE (painted eyes): $100.00.

MARY: $175.00. LAMB with glass eyes: $175.00. DESK: $25.00.

COMIC CHARACTERS: MAX: $175.00. BARNEY GOOGLE: $200.00. JIGGS: $200.00. MAGGIE: $200.00. FELIX THE CAT: Small: $75.00. Large: $100.00.

PICK UP STICKS toy: O. SCHOENHUT, INC. $15.00.

Small Hobo: $100.00. Large Hobo: $175.00.

f Nice Clean Lumber. All parts accurately made to fit together.

PELLER
lves
erly
d
e floor

Reprint from Schoenhut Catalog.

ROLLY-DOLLY TOYS

Patents: Dec. 2, 1902
Apr. 14, 1903
May 17, 1904
Dec. 15, 1908

A great many Rolly-Dolly toys were manufactured between 1902 and 1934 ranging in sixty different sizes and styles. They were sold in department and toy stores throughout the United States, priced from ten cents to a dollar each.

Rolly-Dolly or Rolly-Polly toys were known to be one of the oldest types of toy in history.

They were constructed of paper mache with a brilliant oil color and heavy enamel varnish.

A circular label with the name Schoenhut appeared on the bottom of each of the toys. These were easy to identify without the label.

The Rolly-Dolly is easy to find in the larger size. The smaller ones are a bit harder to obtain.

Reprint from Schoenhut Catalog.

ROLLY DOLLY Toys. Large Baby: $175.00. Small Negro Billikin: $75.00. Small Drummer Boy: $75.00.

SCHOENHUT WOOD DOLLS
From 1911 to 1926

All wood dolls, fully jointed at the neck, shoulders, elbows, wrists, hips, knees and ankles were joined together with steel spring hinges and swivel connections. Rubber cord was used later to cut down expenses.

The heads were modeled of solid basswood. They had a real lifelike expression, not like the dolly face dolls that appeared later. The heads were hand carved by an Italian Noble, Graziano, who was one of the best known sculptors at that time.

All parts were held together tightly and were flexible enough to assume any realistic position or pose. Holes in the sole of the feet and shoes to accommodate a short post on a round metal disc served as a doll stand which went with each doll. The dolls were painted with natural oil colors and could be cleaned with care.

Dolls came with carved hair or with very fine quality mohair wigs. Human hair was never used. Many different character faces were introduced and became instantly popular. The dolls were sold dressed or undressed. All had knitted union suits which ranged in price from $2.00 to $5.00.

It was in 1915 when Miss Dolly Schoenhut was added to the doll line. This doll could do almost everything but eat and talk.

The Schoenhut mannequin was produced the same year, but only 1,000 were made. His body construction was different from the other dolls. It was 22" tall and could bend at the waist. These dolls were also used as artist models.

The Walker doll was introduced in 1917. The heads were the usual carved in eye with the small kissy mouth. However, the bodies were much different than conventional Schoenhut bodies. They were only jointed at the neck. The one piece arms, curved outward, were jointed at the shoulder. The one piece legs were jointed under the body with wooden inserts which enabled the doll's legs to swing freely.

Later as the doll sales dropped, because of the reopening of the import business, a less expensive doll had to be produced and for the first time they cut down expenses by using rubber stringing in place of springs.

In 1924, a cloth bodied mamma doll was produced. Head and hands were made of wood. These dolls, though inexpensive, did not go over as big as the first dolls. This marked the end of the Schoenhut doll production.

Other dolls by O. Schoenhut, Inc., have been made but not at all like the play doll. These dolls were the Clothespin Dolls in 1935. They were interesting in their construction but not too popular. Photographs of these dolls can be seen along with the others.

Dates to Remember:

First Carved Heads and Wigged Dolls	1911
Miss Dolly Schoenhut	1915
Mannequins	1915
Walker Doll	1917
Sleep Eyed Doll with	
Open or Closed Mouth	1921
Wooden Head Shoulder Plate Doll	1924
Composition	1928 to 1934

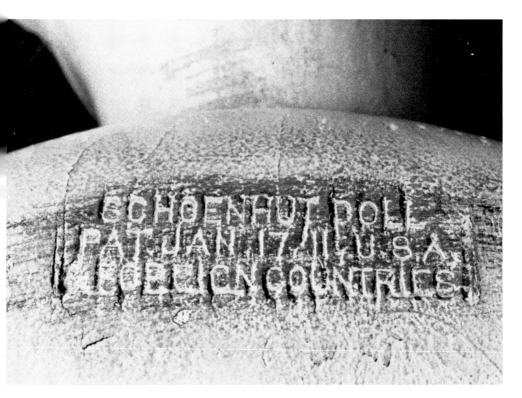

Mark on back of carved hair girl.

Back markings of walking doll. Note patent Applied for stamp not found on most walkers.

Original tin Schoenhut pin that came with each doll.

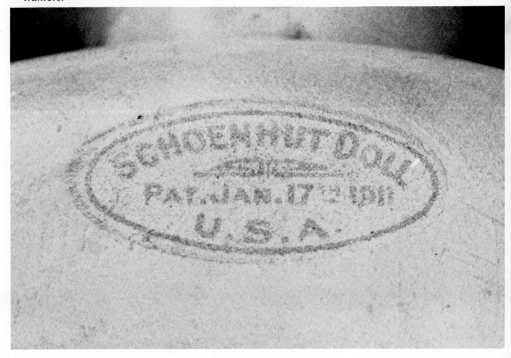

1911 decal mark on shoulders.

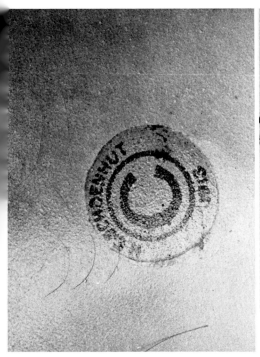

1913 decal mark found on back of heads.

The HARRY E. SCHOENHUT incised mark found on back of heads. Harry was the son of Albert, who later took over the designing department, after graduating from Art School.

12" pouty, 16" Walker, 16" Carved hair boy, 22" Smiling Girl, 16" Carved hair girl. All have original clothes. Note the five different original shoes.

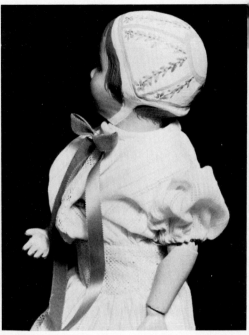

16" "BONNET" Girl. (re-painted), intaglio eyes. $700.00.

Side view of Bonnet Doll.

16" All original carved hair girl with original stand. Intaglio eyes. This was one of the first dolls. $600.00.

Shows back of carved hair girl. All original. $600.00.

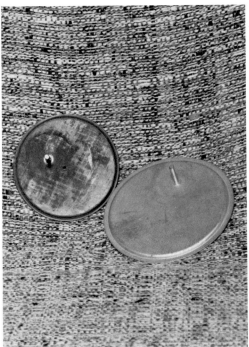

18″ All original Black man. $900.00. Original stand: $5.00.

Original Schoenhut doll stands. Small takes dolls from 12″ to 16″ $10.00. Large: 18″ to 22″ $15.00.

NATURE BABIES: Curved arms and legs. Painted eyes. Pouty mouths. 12″ $275.00. 16″ $325.00.

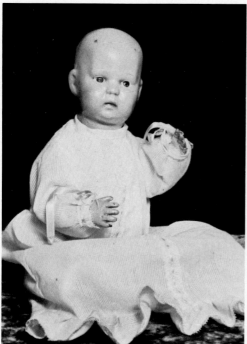

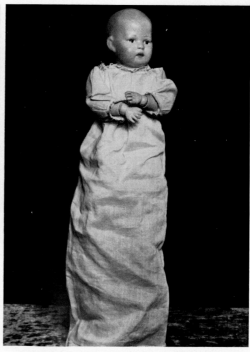

12" NATURE BABY. Painted hair and eyes. Pouty mouth. Ca. 1915. $235.00.

12" Infant with jointed arms and legs. Painted eyes. Pouty. All original. Ca. 1915. $250.00.

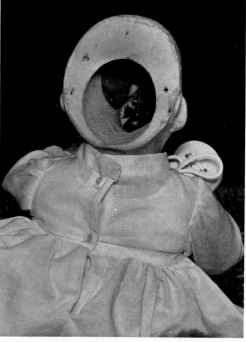

26" Sleep eyed baby with open mouth. $300.00.

Shows inside head of open mouth, sleep eyed baby.

Carved hair, intaglio eyes. Smiling mouth. Pink bow in hair. All original. $500.00.

16″ Carved hair boy with intaglio eyes. Somber face. Original shoes. $450.00.

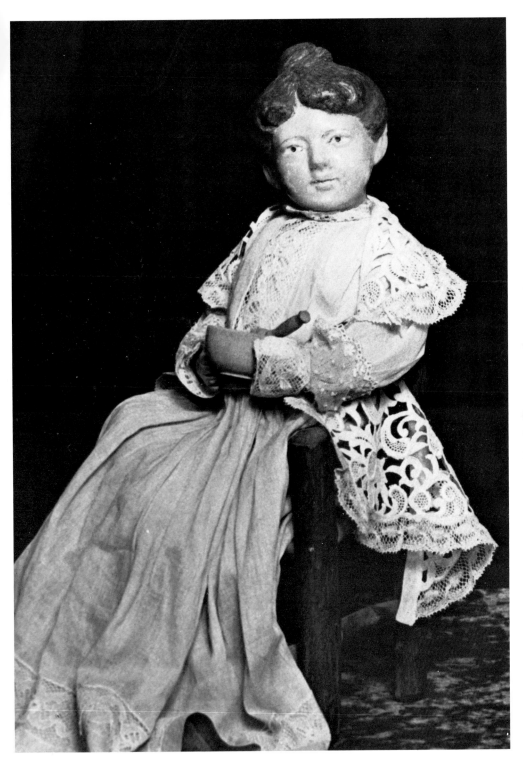

16″ "CARRIE" and referred to as Mother Schoenhut, also shown in Catalog #16/102 as a little girl. $1,000.00.

16" Carved hair girl with carved ribbon, Original box, clothing. $450.00.

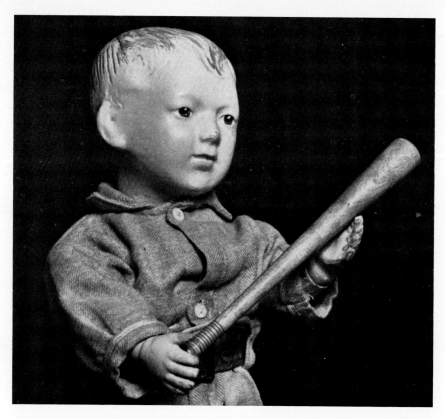

16" All original boy with baseball suit. Carved hair. $650.00.

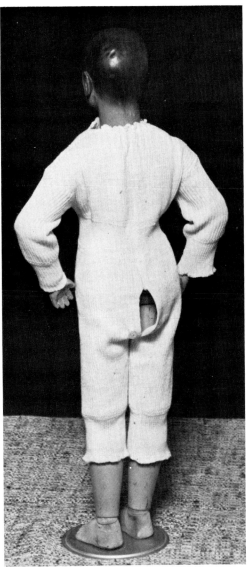

Male Schoenhut doll used for Stetson Hat
ads and is one of a kind. 22″ tall. $1,000.00.

Back view of man.

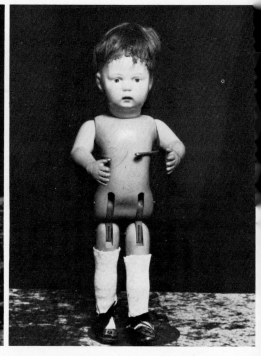

12" Sleep eyed, open mouth baby. $275.00.　　Shows undressed walking doll.

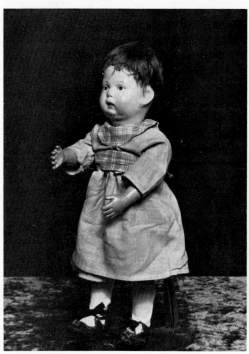

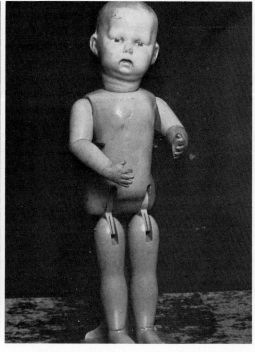

16" All original walking doll with painted eyes and wig. $375.00.

22" Bald head walking doll. Pouty mouth. Painted eyes. $375.00.

12" Painted eyes. Pouty mouth. All original. Note high top leather shoes. $375.00.

12" painted eyed pouty with original wig. $250.00.

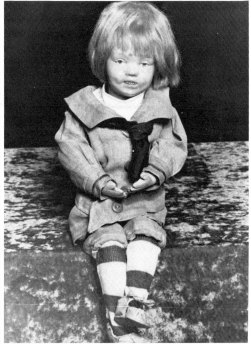

18" Toddler boy. Painted eyes. Very good copy of original shoes. $275.00.

16" Squinty eyes. Smiling mouth with full row of teeth. Dimples in chin and cheeks. $450.00.

14" Intaglio eyes. Wig re-placed. $275.00.

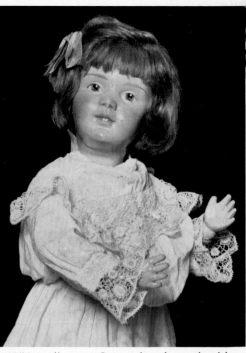

22" Intaglio eyes. Open/closed mouth with two carved teeth. Dimple in chin. Smiling face. All original. $600.00.

22" Sleep eyed girl with carved teeth. $350.00.

16" Pouty with intaglio eyes. Dimple in chin. $375.00.

18" Intaglio eyes (brown). Original wig. $300.00. 3" Felix the Cat $100.00.

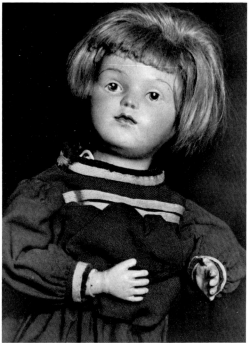

18" Blue intaglio eyes. Original dress. Ca. 1915. $375.00.

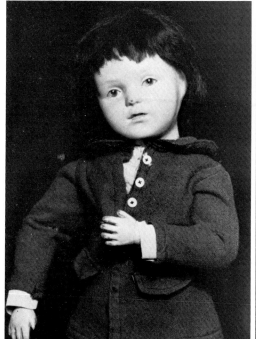

18" Wigged and with brown intaglio eyes. $375.00.

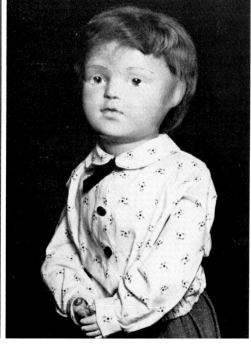

22" Intaglio eyes. Half smiling mouth. $375.00.

22" "DOLLY SCHOENHUT" Carved eyes that look like glass. Smiling mouth with four carved teeth. $300.00.

1935 Clothespin dolls by O. Schoenhut, Inc. $300.00 set.

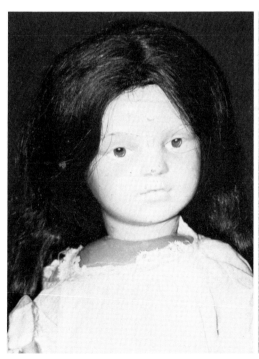

22″ Schoenhut girl with long wig and brown eyes.

Schoenhut Doll Stands

DOLL HOUSES AND TOY APARTMENT HOUSE ROOMS

More success followed the dolls with the addition of Doll Houses and Toy Apartment House Rooms. These were made of wood and fiber board, embossed to resemble stone walls and tiles for the roofs.

The interior was covered with fancy lithographs to give an appearance of wallpaper. The houses were made to open on one or both sides. The front and back remained stationary. Later, in time, houses were made without the back wall.

Small one room Doll House with flower boxes front and sides. Opens at side. $275.00.

The base of the houses was embossed to represent rough stone. The Schoenhut label was found on either side of the base on metal or decal.

In 1927, doll houses with gardens, shrubbery, trees and garages with automobiles were added. The houses were given code names in order to eliminate error in ordering.

The Dess House and Grounds (22" x 36") sold for about $12.00.

The Dooly House and Grounds (29" x 42") sold for about $16.00.

Many other houses were made at that time.

In 1928, a house, one room deep, with a removable front section to make all rooms visible was introduced. This made it easier for a child to re-arrange the furniture.

In 1933, still another much lower priced house without a back wall appeared. They were two stories with one room on each floor and finished in attractive colors.

The Doge House (13" x 8" x 10½") sold for about $1.20.

The Dogna — two stories, four rooms (15″ x 9″ x 12″) sold for $2.00.

The Doily, 17″ x 10″ x 13″ was about $3.00.

As they were being made, materials and construction changed. Fiberboard, with a painted stucco finish in cream or white became popular.

Toy apartment house rooms were added to the line. These had side and back walls, hinged for easy folding. They were made of wood and were well painted inside and out. The rooms varied in size according to the type. Living Rooms: 19¾″ x 8¾″ x 8″; Kitchen: 11¾″ x 8¾″ x 8″; Dining Room: 13¼″ x 8¾″ x 8″; Bedroom: 17⅜″ x 8¾″ x 8″; Bathroom: 9¾″ x 8¾″ x 8″. These rooms could be purchased individually or as a group. The five rooms could be jointed together with strips of white molding. The furniture was sold separately.

The production of the doll houses continued until the A. Schoenhut Company went out of business in 1934.

Doll House showing rooms from side opening.

Large two story, two room Doll House. Opens at one side. $375.00.

Small one-room Doll House. Flower box at front only. Opens at side. $250.00.

DOLL HOUSE FURNITURE

In 1928, the first line of doll house furniture was produced. It was made of hardwood, walnut in color; the bathrooms were white enamel.

Styles changed with the time, and in 1930, along with the conventional furniture, there appeared a doll house sized Schoenhut piano and bench. The living room set changed from walnut color to green or red painted or flocked. Kitchen sets made of wood and painted a pastel green were produced in 1931. The bedroom was changed in color to pastel pink.

More modern colors were used in 1932: orange kitchen sets, orchid bathroom sets, pastel green bedroom sets.

A less expensive and smaller line of furniture in 1933 consisted of six piece living rooms, dining rooms, kitchens, bathrooms and bedrooms.

The last of the doll house furniture in early 1934 shows the change in style with a more modern radio. It had changed from the four legged to floor model console. Also, a change in the kitchen set and a much more modern bathroom.

Late in 1934, a chaise lounge was added to the bedroom, a tea cart for the dining room, a bookcase to the living room, a utility cabinet and a trash container to the kitchen, and a clothes hamper to the bathroom sets.

1934 marked the end of the doll house furniture manufacturing.

Bedroom set with walnut finish. Painted on design. $25.00 per set.

Green enamel Kitchen set: $35.00.

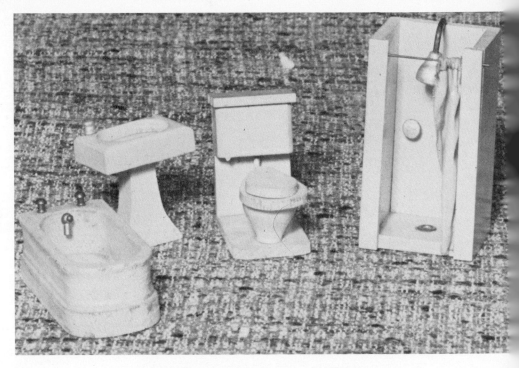

Early bathroom. White enamel. Set: $35.00.

Livingroom set: 4 pc. $25.00.

RAILROAD STATIONS

Not too much can be written about this item because it was not produced in volume.

Railroad stations were introduced along with doll houses in 1923 and were constructed about the same way. They were made in three different sizes.

The largest: (Dahlia) 17½" x 13" x 12½" priced at about $6.00. A one-room structure.

Medium: (Diazolizo) 14" x 9" x 9" priced at about $4.00.

Small: (Diaza) 11" x 7½" x 7½" priced at about $2.50.

Platform houses used with Train Set Villages. They are pre-constructed and not marked. Small: $50.00. Large: $65.00.

Every Child Loves to Build

| CHURCH | SCHOOL HOUSE | HOUSE | RAILROAD STATION | R. R. FREIGHT STATION |

Reprint from Schoenhut Catalog

DELVAN HUMPTY DUMPTY CIRCUS
1950-1952

The Delvan Company was given the rights to reproduce the original Circus in the early 1950's. Although this is not a true Schoenhut Humpty Dumpty Circus, something must be said about it.

A few changes had to be made because of the high cost of production. Clown heads were made of plastic rather than wood. The animals remained about the same, made entirely of wood with the only difference being in the construction. If you pay close attention when comparing the early toy to the later, you will notice the original animals have a single slot under the body where the legs are joined. The Delvan animals have two slots. The later also have the identification stamp Humpty Dumpty Circus under the body of the animals or on the feet of the clowns and cowboys (new caricatures added to the circus).

Comparisons are shown in the picture section of the book.

DELVAN Circus. This is a re-issue of the Schoenhut circus and was made in 1952. Tent and 18 pieces. $500.00.

BIBLIOGRAPHY

Ladies Home Journal
December, 1914
December, 1919
November, 1926

Women's Home Companion, December 1915

Playthings, a Trade Journal published in New York.

INDEX